SECULAR BUDDHISM

Eastern Thought for Western Minds

Noah Rasheta

Copyright © 2016 by Noah Rasheta
All rights reserved, including the right of reproduction in whole or in part in any form.

Bulk discounts available. For details visit:
www.secularbuddhism.com/contact or email
books@secularbuddhism.com

For Rajko, Noelle, and Genevieve.

Contents

Introduction 6

Part One: The Foundation of Understanding

Chapter 1 - The Situation at Hand 11

Chapter 2 - What is Spirituality? 17

Chapter 3 - Spiritual Languages 21

Chapter 4 - What is Truth? 25

Chapter 5 - What is Freedom? 32

Chapter 6 - What are Faith and Doubt? 37

Part Two: The Nature of Reality

Chapter 7 - The Four Noble Truths 46

Chapter 8 - The Eightfold Path 60

Chapter 9 - Seeing With I's of Wisdom 72

Chapter 10 - Awareness and Emptiness 79

Chapter 11 - The Karma of You 87

Chapter 12 - Life Before Death 91

Chapter 13 - Becoming Who You Are 99

Conclusion 107

Introduction

"The secret of Buddhism is to remove all ideas, all concepts, in order for the truth to have a chance to penetrate, to reveal itself." - Thich Nhat Hanh

We see and experience reality through our own unique lens of understanding. This lens of understanding is influenced by when and where we live (time and space). Collectively, our ideas and concepts about reality ultimately influence how we experience life. Therefore, our ideas, beliefs, and concepts (most of which aren't even ours, but are inherited) will determine our perceived reality. This means that in terms of space and time, the "me" of here and now is going to experience reality differently than the "me" of another place or time. The essence of Buddhism is to discover that there are two realities: reality the way it is and reality the way we think it is. Buddhism is often referred to as the path of liberation: the liberation from the ideas and concepts that keep us from seeing reality as it is.

Here's a simple example. A few years ago, I had to bring on a new supplier for a special product my photography gear company was working on, called a Gimbal (basically a stabilizer to keep smartphone video steadier). I connected with Chris, the head of sales at the new supplier's factory, to work on prototyping the Gimbal virtually. After several months of emailing back and forth, we needed to meet in person. But when I got to the meeting place, I didn't see Chris anywhere.

I checked my email and confirmed that I was in the right place at the right time, which I was. Maybe Chris was running late. I waited a few minutes. No Chris. I waited a few more minutes. Still no Chris. By now I was pacing back and forth, impatiently wondering "where is he?"

Finally, I sat down on a bench near me, where two young women were also sitting, and pulled out my phone to call Chris and ask what was taking him so long. Before I could do that, one of the girls turned around and said "Hi, are you Noah? I'm Chris!" I started laughing, and when I told her why I was cracking up, she laughed too. (And yes, Chris and HER company manufacture all of our Gimbals now.)

Aside from being a funny story about me, the Chris story is a story that exemplifies just how beliefs can affect our understanding of reality. I believed that Chris was a man, so I thought he wasn't at our meeting place on time (and was kind of a jerk for being late). It never occurred to me that Chris might be right where she was supposed to be, because I thought she was a he! My inaccurate belief blinded me to the reality of the situation.

How many realities are we blind to simply because we already hold an idea, concept, or belief that prevents us from seeing reality as it is? Like trying to pour tea into a cup that's already full, we approach reality with preconceived beliefs of what it should be, then wonder why we struggle to deal with how it really is. There isn't room for new awareness or understanding in a mind already filled with ideas and beliefs. In many cases, our ideas and beliefs are the very source of the suffering that we're trying to reduce. As you read through this book, I invite you to pause and evaluate the ideas and beliefs you currently hold. You may find that some of them stand between you and seeing what was in front of you all along.

In this book, I will present some of the key teachings found in Buddhism regarding the nature of reality. My goal is to present these teachings in a secular language—not as a religion, but as a way of life, not as something to believe in but as something to notice or observe. I write these pages with one of my favorite quotes by the Dalai Lama in mind: "do not try to use what you learn from Buddhism to be a Buddhist; use it to be a better whatever-you-already-are." The world doesn't need more Buddhists, it needs more mindful human beings, believers and non-believers alike. This book is not an attempt to proselytize or convert anyone to Buddhism. The principles of mindful living can benefit anyone. Imagine a world with more mindful politicians, religious leaders, and teachers; more mindful bosses and employees, bankers and investors, writers and salespeople and doctors and attorneys. My only goal with writing this book is to spread the teachings of mindfulness in a vernacular that can be accepted and understood by all.

Part One: The Foundation of Understanding

Chapter One: The Situation at Hand

There is parable in early Buddhist texts called "The Parable of the Arrow" that illustrates the pragmatic approach of Buddhist thought regarding the nature of reality. A certain monk was troubled by the fact that he did not have the answers to life's existential questions. Did I exist before life? Do I exist after death? Etc. He was so troubled by the fact that the Buddha had not given answers to life's existential questions that he finally approached the Buddha and threatened to abandon his monastic vows unless he could get satisfactory answers. The Buddha answered:

It's just as if a man were wounded with an arrow thickly smeared with poison. His friends &

companions, kinsmen & relatives would provide him with a surgeon, and the man would say, 'I won't have this arrow removed until I know whether the man who wounded me was a noble warrior, a priest, a merchant, or a worker.' He would say, 'I won't have this arrow removed until I know the given name & clan name of the man who wounded me... until I know whether he was tall, medium, or short... until I know whether he was dark, ruddy-brown, or golden-colored... until I know his home village, town, or city... until I know whether the bow with which I was wounded was a long bow or a crossbow... until I know whether the bowstring with which I was wounded was fiber, bamboo threads, sinew, hemp, or bark... until I know whether the shaft with which I was wounded was wild or cultivated... until I know whether the feathers of the shaft with which I was wounded were those of a vulture, a stork, a hawk, a peacock, or another bird... until I know whether the shaft with which I was wounded was bound with the sinew of an ox, a water buffalo, a langur, or a monkey.' He would say, 'I won't have this arrow removed until I know whether the shaft with which I was wounded was that of a common arrow, a curved arrow, a barbed, a calf-toothed, or an oleander arrow.' **The man would die and those things would still remain unknown to him.**

This parable is about "the situation at hand." In the parable, the situation at hand is that a man has been shot by an arrow. The greater teaching is that in life, difficulties arise and people suffer. In the parable, the wise thing to do is to remove the arrow instead of spending time and energy focusing on who shot it, what kind of arrow it was, how it was poisoned, etc. Like the man in the parable, we humans have a tendency to want to search for answers to questions that are frankly irrelevant, rather than addressing our situation(s) at hand and removing our personal arrows. Where did we come from? Why are we here? What happens to us when we die? These are some of the existential questions that can get in the way of attending to the situation at hand. Rather than attempting to answer existential questions, Buddhism asks us to look inward and ask ourselves: "why do I feel the need to know these things that are unknowable?" The situation at hand for each and every one of us, is that we are all struck with an arrow, we all experience suffering, and our time is limited. What do we do with the situation at hand? Perhaps it would be wise to remove the arrow that's causing our suffering and focus less on the aspects of the arrow itself. At base, those aspects are irrelevant to the situation at hand.

This parable is significant here because an important lesson of Buddhism is that it is not concerned with immense, unknowable, metaphysical questions. Especially in this book, where we'll explore Buddhism from a secular angle, we will not be asking the kinds of existential questions listed above. We won't be examining what kind of arrows we've been collectively shot with; we'll be discussing how to take the arrows out and live healthier, happier, and more fulfilling lives by doing so. In other words, secular Buddhism is the parable of the situation at hand brought to life.

To more closely explore our situation at hand through the Buddhist perspective, we need to understand that some concepts we'll encounter have different meanings in Eastern thought than in Western thought. Words like truth, spirituality, faith, and other similar words mean different things to someone who was raised in a 21st century Judeo-Christian western society vs what the author meant when using that word centuries before half way around the world. The Buddhist or Eastern understanding of these words and concepts can be quite different from what we Westerners typically understand them to mean. So it will be helpful to start out by explaining what many of these common concepts mean when used in the context of Buddhist teachings. By understanding the meaning of the words now, we will grasp them more effectively later when we hear them being used in the explanations of Buddhist philosophy and concepts.

Oftentimes, these words can trigger negative emotions or feelings for the secular-minded. I struggled with some of these concepts myself when I was first studying Buddhism. In the experience of searching for Chris (the man), I simply couldn't see Chris (the woman, the real Chris. So it was with trying to understand words like faith from a secular and/or Buddhist standpoint while struggling with the more traditional, religious, and/or Western definition I had for faith. It's alright if some of these words are difficult to hear at first, and even if they trigger you a bit. Take your time in exploring them, and be kind to yourself if and when they bring up difficult feelings. I only ask that you be open to understanding these terms through the Buddhist lens, since they will create some of the mental foundation for understanding secular Buddhism and using it to remove your own arrows.

Chapter 2: What is Spirituality?

Carl Sagan had this say about spirituality in his book "The Demon-Haunted World":

"Spirit" comes from the Latin word "to breathe." What we breathe is air, which is certainly matter, however thin. Despite usage to the contrary, there is no necessary implication in the word "spiritual" that we are talking of anything other than matter (including the matter of which the brain is made), or anything outside the realm of science. On occasion, I will feel free to use the word. **Science is not only compatible with spirituality; it is a profound source of spirituality.** *When we recognize our place in an immensity of light years and in the passage of ages, when we grasp the intricacy, beauty and subtlety of life, then that soaring feeling, that sense of elation and humility combined, is surely spiritual. So are our emotions in the presence of great art or music or literature, or of acts of exemplary selfless courage such as those of Mohandas Gandhi or Martin Luther King Jr.* **The notion that science**

and spirituality are somehow mutually exclusive does a disservice to both."

That sense of awe and wonder that we all experience, whether it be through scientific understanding or through religious understanding, is universal. We all feel incredibly small when confronted with the vastness of the cosmos, or when simply standing in nature. In these moments, we feel a form of spirituality.

Spirituality is really just a combination of two things: connection and meaning.
Connection: There is a sense of awe and wonder when we connect with something greater than ourselves. For some, this comes through the understanding that there is a greater force in the universe, a deity, a creator. Many religious narratives provide a sense of connection to something greater than ourselves. Science can evoke many of the same feelings. I remember watching the show Cosmos with Neil deGrasse Tyson (a modern version of Carl Sagan's original Cosmos) and feeling an overwhelming sense of awe as I tried to grasp my smallness in terms of space and time. I remember feeling a tremendous sense of connection to everything.

Learning about the cosmos felt like a spiritual experience to me.

Meaning: Where does our sense of meaning come from? We tend to look for meaning in life as if it was something out there, outside of ourselves, that if we look hard enough, we can find it and keep it. Some find meaning through the arts: painting, singing, dancing, writing, etc. Others find meaning through religious devotion. Some find meaning in the pursuit of happiness or the pursuit of fame, fortune, or power. Most of us probably find meaning in a mix of several things. Plus, the meaning we find in life will evolve and change over time. Our sense of meaning as a college student will probably be quite different from our sense of meaning as a grandparent.

A spiritual path is the path that leads a person to feeling a sense of connection and meaning in life. There may be many spiritual paths, religious and non-religious. So any experience that makes us feel more connected or gives meaning to our lives can be considered a spiritual experience. In this sense, spirituality doesn't have to have anything to do with religion, dogma, or beliefs. When we seek connection and meaning, we're on a spiritual path. And when the words "spiritual" or "spirituality" appear in this book, you can take them to mean "connection" and/or "meaning."

Chapter 3: Spiritual Languages

Several years ago I read Gary Chapman's book *The Five Love Languages*. This book outlines the five most common ways that people communicate and experience love: gifts, quality time, words of affirmation, acts of service (devotion), and physical touch (intimacy). As a newlywed at the time, it was extremely helpful to learn that my wife and I actually spoke different love languages. Until then, I had just assumed that my understanding and experience of love was universal and that everyone else experienced it the same way as I did, or at least they should. I was surprised to discover that something as universal as love is actually expressed and experienced very differently for different people. My primary love language is physical touch and my wife's is acts of service. I assumed that cuddling or holding hands while sitting on the couch was a perfectly acceptable way of expressing my affection (it was for me), but I was surprised to find out that washing the dishes or offering to help around the house was a much more powerful expression of love for her, because her primary love language is acts of service. Knowing that my wife has a different primary love language than mine has allowed us to improve our ability to communicate and express love with each other in meaningful ways.

Similar to the concept of love languages, I believe we each have "spiritual languages" as well, different forms of communicating and experiencing our senses of connection and meaning. Spending time with family, being in nature, practicing rituals, and holding specific beliefs are all spiritual languages. This wide variety of spiritual languages can help us understand why someone could feel comfortable on a spiritual path that is highly dogmatic or a path that is steeped in rituals, while someone else can feel just as connected while on a secular path that is devoid of religious practices. Both would be experiencing connection and meaning. It's important to recognize that others may be on a spiritual path that is more suited for them than our own would be, and it would be unhealthy and unwise to expect everyone to be on the same spiritual path.

Generally, we each inherit our spiritual/religious views from our family and from the society or culture in which we live. This is why most people will stick to their inherited faith tradition throughout their entire lives. But not everyone will remain on their inherited spiritual path, and often one of the reasons people do so is that the path no longer speaks their spiritual language. The path they started on no longer provides that sense of connection and meaning that they, like all of us, naturally long for. If we struggle to find connection and meaning on a particular spiritual path, it is natural for us to look for it on another, just as a person who dislikes receiving gifts may instead explore physical touch or words of affirmation as a primary love language.

Spiritual languages can also change and evolve over time. My preferred ways of understanding and experiencing connection and meaning have changed over the years, and I've observed the same thing in almost everyone I know. I've even observed this with people who stay within one single faith tradition their whole life: the way they understand their faith, the reasons for their devotion to it, even the language they use around it may change, even though their spiritual path, faith tradition, or religious home remains the same. Some people even leave a particular spiritual path for a number of years, only to decide to return to it at a different point in their lives.

As a side note, there is a fascinating TED Talk by British journalist Johann Hari titled "Everything You Think You Know About Addiction is Wrong". In his talk, Hari discusses the research into the underlying causes of addiction and concludes that the opposite of addiction is not sobriety but connection. This research implies that perhaps a cause of addiction is our inability to have healthy sense of connection. This research makes me wonder if inadvertently push ourselves and other people down unhealthy paths because we have been taught for too long that there is only one proper or true spiritual path. What might it be like for our senses of spirituality if all forms of connection and meaning were welcomed and accepted?

Chapter 4: What is Truth?

"Declarations of high confidence mainly tell you that an individual has constructed a coherent story in his mind, not necessarily that the story is true." - Daniel Kahneman

There are two categories of truths: empirical truths (natural truths) and conceptual truths (man-made truths). Empirical truths are true *regardless* of human beliefs. These are typically truths that can be tested and proven through the scientific method. I like to imagine these as the truths that would still apply even if there were never any humans on the planet. These are the truths we typically find in nature, things like gravity, natural selection, the laws of physics, etc. Conceptual truths, on the other hand, are true *because* of human beliefs. These truths exist because of humans and the concepts we've created.

There are two types of conceptual truths. Religions, the rule of law, cultural norms and customs, and the structures that make up society create (and/or are created by) one type of conceptual truths, known as *shared conceptual truths*. Others form in our minds as we get to know ourselves as human beings. These are called *personal conceptual truths*.

An example of a shared conceptual truth is that gold is more valuable than silver. This is a conceptual truth because it depends on humanity to be true. If there were no more people on Earth, gold and silver would have no value at all. It's a shared conceptual truth because it's true outside of my personal sphere. It's not just something I believe, it's something everyone believes, and it's true because society as a whole accepts that it is true.

Shared conceptual truths are important because our ability to create and maintain civilization depends on our ability to coexist and work together. Political, economic, and religious systems all work because of shared beliefs in conceptual truths—that killing and stealing are wrong, for example, or that a dollar bill is worth a dollar, or that a red light means stop. It allows us to place authority and trust in public figures, because we share the truth that their positions have responsibility for us. It even allows us to determine our nationalities, since we share the conceptual truths of national borders and cultures.

A personal conceptual truth would be a truth that is true for me personally because of my belief in it. It would not be true if I did not exist. Some personal truths sound a lot like opinions: hot dogs are gross, eggs taste better with hot sauce, math isn't fun, blue is a nicer color than green, etc. In fact, that's often what an opinion is: a personal truth for you that may not be true for anyone else. Then there are deeper personal truths that involve how we see ourselves: I'm smart, I'm stupid, I'm important, what I say doesn't matter, etc. Like all personal truths, these are true because you believe them—and sometimes, believing them can be harmful. It's easy to get bent out of shape over mere ideas in your head, if you've accepted them as personal truths.

Personal truths are important because everyone has them. Your personal truths are part of your selfhood, just as my personal truths are part of mine. But everyone's personal truths are different, even if they relate to the same things. It's like the parable of the six blind men and the elephant. In this parable, six blind men approach an elephant, touch it in a different place, and begin to describe it based on where they touch it. One describes the tail while the other describes the trunk, another the leg, and another the ears, etc. All six are certain that their experience of having felt the elephant is the accurate and correct interpretation while failing to understand that the other descriptions were also correct—and that their own descriptions were also incorrect, since they each only felt one part of the elephant. Our unique perspectives will determine our truths. (Incidentally, this applies to not only individuals but also to groups. If a whole group experiences the trunk of the elephant, they will all be certain that the description of the tail is wrong and they will reassure each other that their accurate description of the trunk is right. This is sometimes known as groupthink or mob mentality.)

Finally, there are personal truths that depend on individual experience. As an identical twin, I was often asked while growing up, "what is it like to be a twin?" I used to try to describe what it's like but as I've gotten older, I've realized that it's impossible to convey the answer. The truth of what it's like to be a twin can only be understood by being a twin. Being a twin for me is a lot like what *not* being a twin is probably like for you (assuming you're not a twin). Being in love is another example. If you've ever been in love, imagine going back in time to before you were in love and trying to tell yourself what it will be like to be in love. The old you wouldn't be able to understand. Or parenthood—nothing prepared me for what it was like to experience fatherhood except fatherhood. The first time I held my newborn baby in my arms, it was in that precise moment that I knew what it was like to be a dad. If I tried to go back in time and explain what that would be like to my younger self, it would be impossible to convey the experience. My explanation would only create a concept for my younger self to try to imagine.

One last point about truth being relative and defined by our experiences can be found in Plato's allegory of the cave. In this famous story, we learn about some prisoners who have been trapped in a cave their whole lives, having never seen the world outside of the cave. They are chained in such a way that they are facing the wall, with their backs towards the entrance of the cave. Due to their positioning, they can occasionally see shadows on the cave wall of the things that are passing by the cave. They occasionally hear noises and they associate the sounds with the shadows they see. They only know the world through the shadows they see on the cave wall. One day, one of the prisoners escapes and leaves the cave. At first he can't see anything because it's too bright and he's blinded by the brightness. Over time his eyes adjust and he can see things with much more clarity than before. For the first time he's seeing things as they really are. From that moment, he understands that the shadow of a thing is not the same as the thing itself. Elated with his new understanding of the world, he returns to the cave to tell his friends all about what he's seen but to his surprise, they don't believe him. It's not that they don't want to believe him but they literally can't believe him. They are simply not capable. They only know the world through the shadows and they've never experienced life any other way.

We must strive to experience reality as it is for ourselves so that we can have an experiential understanding of this reality, rather than just a conceptual understanding of it.

Chapter 5: What is Freedom?

Buddhism is often referred to as the path of liberation. But what does liberation or freedom mean on the spiritual path? Freedom is a relative thing, it's generally freedom *to* or freedom *from*. Imagine a prisoner who has recently obtained freedom (like the one who escaped the cave in the previous chapter). This prisoner is now free *from* the confines of the prison cell and the prison walls. He is also free *to* walk freely on the street, to walk into a store and purchase something, to eat in a restaurant, etc. In our lives we are free to work a job, marry, raise a family, adopt or leave a religion, etc. We are also free from things like censorship of our speech, denial of free assembly, and fear of being hit by a car when we cross the street at a crosswalk.

But in a spiritual sense, freedom looks different. Spiritually, we are all prisoners. We are bound by our conceptual truths, ideas, and beliefs. When we live in a society that portrays a certain body image as the "ideal" image, for example, and we collectively or personally believe that idea to be true, it can become a real source of suffering. I imagine that we all know someone who has a negative image of their body. Can you see how the conceptual truth of what an ideal body is can become a mental prison for anyone who believes it? They believe that since their body doesn't look like the societal ideal, they are imperfect, broken, ugly. They become trapped in a mental prison of their own making, where their own thoughts reinforce negative self-images.

Spiritual freedom, then, is freedom from our own beliefs. And the most important step towards freedom/liberation is to *understand* that it is our own beliefs that bind us. We can take a close look at our personal conceptual truths and analyze these truths to see if they are causing suffering to ourselves or to others. It's often difficult to recognize the difference between personal conceptual truth and reality, though. We create stories and meaning around reality, which ultimately can create two realities: the reality of what is, and the reality of the story we've created around what is.

Imagine you are driving on the freeway

and suddenly, without warning, someone cuts you off. You are forced to slam on your brakes to avoid hitting them. Then they suddenly do the same to enter the next lane to get around another car and speed off. How do you feel? Most of us feel anger and rage. We think things like "Who does this guy think he is?" and "How dare he cut me off like that?" and probably many other thoughts that I can't print in this book.

Here's the thing though. The anger we feel around this situation has nothing to do with the situation itself, and everything to do with the story we tell ourselves about it. When another driver behaves this way toward us, we tell ourselves that he's a jerk, he treats people badly, he's rude, etc. But what if his wife is in the back seat of the car because she just went into labor? Or what if he just got a call that his child is in the hospital? Those are different stories that could be equally true in this scenario. And if they are, we stop caring about getting cut off because we know this guy needs to get where he's going, fast!

We don't know which, if any, of those stories is true. All we know is what happened: a driver cut us off and then sped away. But if we understand the difference between what happened and the story we tell ourselves about what happened, we can decide how to respond instead of letting our emotions drive our reaction.

This is what freedom from beliefs and concepts ultimately looks like. Victor Frankl, a holocaust survivor and the author of *Man's Search For Meaning*, talks about how there is a space between the stimulus and our response, and in that space we have the freedom to act. This is the sense of freedom that is important on the spiritual path. There is no freedom in reactivity. So next time you get cut off by a seemingly crazy driver, you can find that space between what happens and how you respond or react, and come up with 2-3 alternate stories to what you think is going on. Notice how the change in story can change your emotional reaction. Notice how you feel more freedom in that moment. This will take some practice, but it will get easier each time you do it.

This is the kind of freedom that Buddhism can help anyone achieve, whether they consider themselves secular or spiritual. When we disconnect our emotional reactions from what happens to us, we become free to be better workers, better parents, better partners, better bosses, better human beings.

Chapter 6: What are Faith and Doubt?

Alan Watts talks about how "the attitude of faith is to let go of what we think is true and be open to things as they really are, even though we don't know." Let's revisit the example from the last chapter, where a driver cuts you off. We know now that our emotional reaction comes from a story we tell ourselves about the driver, and that by seizing the moment between event and reaction we can foil the emotional outburst by proposing a few other stories that might be equally true. But there's an objection to this practice that also came up around that event: you don't know which (if any) of those stories are true. You know you got cut off, but you don't *really* know what's happening in that car. Maybe that guy's wife is having a baby in the back seat, or maybe he really is just a jerk. Faith is trusting the unknown and unknowable aspects of our reality while at the same time questioning the story we've created. I don't know if this guy is a jerk or if he's having a medical emergency, but that's okay. I can choose to just be with this event and let it be what it is.

The word "faith" is understood differently in western societies. We believe that having faith means having faith in something or someone, usually a belief or idea that we can't prove or don't see any evidence for. We don't know with certainty if that idea or truth is real, but we want it to be real (or are taught that it's real), so we have faith that it is. This understanding of faith is the foundation of most Western religions, and it's what most people think of when they hear the word "faith" in any context.

From the Buddhist perspective, faith is simply the attitude of being open to whatever may be, and not attaching to an idea or belief of how we want or expect things to be. Imagine you're standing at the edge of a cliff and holding a tree branch to get a better view. Then the branch breaks, tumbling you over the cliff. As you're falling, you notice that you have a tight grip on the broken tree branch that is now falling with you. At some point during the fall, it may occur to you that you're falling no matter what, and clutching the tree branch does nothing for you. You can let go of the branch and it won't change the fact that you're already falling. Buddhism teaches that in life difficulties will arise and we will experience suffering. Holding tight to our ideas is a lot like holding on to the branch--it doesn't change the fact of the situation at hand.

Here's a happier example: think about the game of Tetris. If you grew up in the 1980s or 1990s, you've probably played this object-stacking puzzle game (maybe even a lot!), but if not, all you need to know is that it was the predecessor to games like Candy Crush. It had several different shapes that appeared at random, and you had a few seconds to stack them without any gaps to win the game.

Life is like a game of Tetris! We never know what shape is going to pop up next. In the game of life, things will show up (successes, failures, and everything in between) and when they do, we have limited control with how we can rotate and make these things fit into our current life but before we know it, another thing will show up, and this process goes on and on until the game is over. That's it! It would be silly to play Tetris and yell at the game every time it produces a new shape that we didn't want or didn't need. But in life, we do this all the time. We think that the shapes that showed up are not fair, or we didn't deserve them. We only want the things we want and we don't want the things we don't want. The desire to get only shapes we want and the aversion to the shapes we don't want is poisonous. The certainty of uncertainty is a part of the game. We can learn to develop a sense of trust or faith in ourselves, in our ability to adapt as the game unfolds. As Koyo Kubose likes to say: "Wisdom is nothing more than the attitude of adaptability."

Like faith, doubt also plays an important role on the spiritual path. And like faith, doubt is understood quite differently in western society. Typically, we're told not to doubt, that doubt is a bad or negative thing and that it hurts our faith. We may even be told that doubt is the opposite of faith. From a Buddhist perspective, this is not true. Doubt is just as valuable as faith in our understanding of life.

The Buddhist question is not *whether* to doubt, the question is *what* to doubt. Doubting yourself, your capabilities, your courage, your prospects, etc., is not a good use of doubt. That kind of doubt actually can undermine your faith in yourself. Avoid it. But do doubt the meanings and stories you assign to different events. Doubt that the man cutting you off in traffic is a jerk. Doubt that his wife is giving birth in the back seat. Get comfortable with doubting the stories that pop into your head.

Here's an example of healthy doubt: the Daoist parable of the horse.

An old farmer who's out working in the field when out of the blue a horse appears. His neighbor comes running over and exclaims, "how fortunate you are! A horse has appeared out of nowhere and now it's yours!" The old man simply replies "who knows what is good and what is bad?" The following day, the old man comes out to discover that the horse has broken out of the corral and has run away. The neighbor comes running over and exclaims, "how unfortunate for you, your horse is now gone!" The old man simply replies "who knows what it good and what is bad?" Later that day the horse shows up in the field with four additional horses, and now the neighbor comes running over and exclaims, "how fortunate for you! You got your horse back and now you have all these additional horses too!" To which the old man simply replies, "who knows what is good and what is bad?" Later the old man's son is riding one of the horses, falls off the horse and breaks his leg. The neighbor comes running over and says "how unfortunate, your only son, now with a broken leg, this is so unfortunate!" The old man simply replies, "who knows what is good and what is bad?" The next day, the army comes to town to conscript all the young men to join the army for the war, and they can't take the old man's son because of his broken leg. The neighbor comes running over and says "how fortunate for you, my son was taken but yours has a broken leg and because of that..." Then he pauses and simply says, together with the old man, "who knows what is good and what is bad?"

I love this story because it teaches us a valuable lesson about the dangers of assigning meaning. This story isn't about emotions. I have no doubt that the old man was excited when the horse showed up and probably sad when it left and definitely sad when his son broke his leg, but what's important here is that he was careful to not assign inherent meaning to these events. This is a good example of the reality of what is vs the story we create around what is. The old man was playing the game of Tetris, he was simply working with whatever shape showed up and doing his best with it. He was not numb to emotions like happiness or sadness. He was able to see the space between the stimulus and the reaction and therefore had the freedom to choose how to react to each event instead of being bound by habitual reactivity to each event.

So when we talk about doubting, we want to doubt the meaning that we assign to things. "Who knows what is good and what is bad?" is an example of living with doubt. I simply don't know what is good and what is bad, so I go on playing the game of life with faith in my ability to adapt to whatever will show up next and doubting anytime I find myself attaching meaning to the events as they unfold. We should continually doubt the meaning we attach to things until we, like the farmer's neighbor, can finally pause and simply say "who knows what is good and what is bad?"

Part Two: The Nature of Reality

Now that we have an understanding of the key concepts and meanings we can take a look at several of the main teachings that look into the nature of reality. Remember the situation at hand? In life difficulties arise and we experience suffering. The overall goal of Buddhist teachings is to minimize or alleviate suffering. We can't alleviate something we don't understand properly.

Chapter 7: The Four Noble Truths

One of the foundational teachings in Buddhism relates to what are known as the four noble truths or the four truths for those who would be noble. These are the teachings regarding the nature of suffering. They consist of a simple, direct analysis of the challenges and possibilities of the human condition. These teachings form the core of all Buddhist paths and traditions. These teachings are structured in terms of a medical practice:

1. Diagnose the problem:
   There is suffering
2. Identify the underlying causes:
   The causes of suffering
3. Determine the prognosis:
   Suffering can be ended
4. Prescribe a course of treatment:
   The path to end suffering

The First Noble Truth: There is Suffering

What is the problem? The problem is that in life, difficulties arise, and we suffer. It's not a matter of if, it's a matter of when. Sickness, old age, and death are the obvious "biggies" but there are so many other countless difficulties in life. From losing your job or losing a loved one to being stuck at a red light when you're late to work or dropping your phone and cracking the screen, and on and on. These difficulties cause us to experience suffering. The nature of reality is that difficulties will arise. In life, there is suffering.

Suffering is not personal. It's not a result of who we are or what we do. We don't deserve it, but neither do we deserve not to experience it. It is simply part of the experience of existence. And we will go through it no matter how hard we try not to. Whether we search for a magic formula to remove suffering, chase after money to buy it off or fame to drown it out, or we pray, meditate, or perform rituals to shield ourselves from it, suffering in some form will find us. It is the problem of human existence.

This diagnosis is universal. It's not just you, it's all of us. We're all experiencing difficulties in life. The rich, the famous, the powerful, the pious, everyone! If you think you're alone with your difficulties, spend some time talking to others and ask them about their problems. You'll soon discover that everyone has difficulties. We all have our own difficulties in life that we're contending with.

Imagine that you are about to start a hike or a walk through the woods. Right before you go, I warn you that someone is hiding along the path, dressed in a scary costume and jumping out to scare people. Now that you know, you'll be on the lookout…but the hike is long and at times you forget. The moment the guy in the scary costume jumps out to scare you, you'll still be startled and you'll jump. But you'll recover quicker because you'll remember that you were warned. You'll say to yourself "I knew this was going to happen at some point." Now imagine the same hike but you were never warned about the person in the scary costume. How much scarier might it feel, and how much longer might it take you to recover? This is essentially what Buddhism teaches us about suffering. It's there and it's scary and at some point it's going to jump out to scare you, but instead of saying "life's not fair" or "why is this happening to me?" now you'll remember "I was told that this could happen. I'm not alone, others are also experiencing this same thing albeit in other forms (other scary costumes)." Once you know that suffering is part of the experience, you can accept that it will happen at some point, worry less about it, and be prepared to recover more quickly when it does.

In many Buddhist traditions, suffering is categorized into three main types: the suffering of suffering (physical pain), the suffering of change (emotional loss or grief), and all pervasive suffering (suffering we inflict on ourselves. To illustrate these types, imagine a young kid in high school who's been saving up money for a new motorcycle. He's been hitching rides with friends and with parents all year and is eager to be able to get around on his own. After working all summer, he finally goes and buys a shiny brand new motorcycle. Ecstatic, he decides to go show all his friends his new motorcycle, but on the way there, he accidentally runs into the back of a car that was stopped at the light.

First, he is thrown from the bike onto the pavement, He breaks one arm and gets pretty bad road rash scrapes from the asphalt. His physical pain is *the suffering of suffering*.

Next he looks up and sees his brand-new motorcycle completely mangled and wrecked. He's heartbroken at the loss of his new motorcycle that he worked so hard to save up for. His grief is the second type of suffering, *the suffering of change*.

As he's carried off in the ambulance he starts to think about his friends and what they'll think of him. "They'll think I'm such an idiot", he mumbles to himself. "Now I'm back to being a loser who has to ask everyone for rides." This self-inflicted mental pain is the third suffering type, *pervasive suffering*.

The first two examples of suffering are inevitable and completely natural. The pain that we feel from illness/injury or the pain we experience at the loss of a loved one (or a motorcycle) are completely natural and healthy. We certainly don't love experiencing them, and we may be frightened or angry when they show up unexpectedly, but we know they are part of life. But self-inflicted suffering is not natural or healthy. The purpose of the secular Buddhist path is to help identify and eliminate the self-inflicted suffering that we experience due to our own ignorance. As we move forward in this book, the suffering I will be referring to is pervasive suffering, the type that is self-inflicted.

What the Buddha is trying to teach with this first noble truth is that life is going to be easier for us when we truly understand that suffering is a part of life (for EVERYONE) and there is no way around it. No matter what we do, we can't avoid the sudden and unexpected surprises that will inevitably come our way.

The Second Noble Truth: The Cause of Suffering

Suffering of suffering and suffering of change have no causes. They simply are. Self-inflicted or pervasive suffering, however, has a cause. Generally speaking, we don't suffer because of our circumstances, we suffer because of the way we interpret and perceive those circumstances as they unfold. As we saw in earlier chapters, we habitually react to life as it unfolds, telling ourselves stories that ascribe meaning to events, wondering why difficult things happen to us, wishing things were different, etc.

This is the cause of suffering: *suffering emerges when we want life to be other than it is.* We get frustrated when the world doesn't behave the way we expect it to or the way we think it should and that causes us to react. We want life to conform to our expectations, and we experience suffering when it doesn't. To make matters worse, we're often blind to the fact that the suffering we're experiencing is completely self-inflicted. This becomes a vicious cycle, because the more we feel this sense of suffering, the more we reinforce the very cause of it: wanting life to be other than it is. The more intense the suffering, the more we want to be rid of it, but the more we want to be rid of it, the more intense the suffering will be.

There are three important reasons we fall victim to self-inflicted suffering: ignorance, desire, and aversion. In Buddhist teachings these are known as the three poisons. They are habits of how we relate to our experiences, and they are often so deeply ingrained that they cloud our perspectives without our even knowing they're there.

Ignorance represents all the things that we don't know that we don't know. It's also our inability to see the difference between reality (what is), and our own stories. Remember how difficult it can be for us to just see things as they are because we are continually creating stories and making meaning out of what happens to us.

Desire is everything that we think that we want. This is our habit of desiring things that we think will eliminate our suffering. Oftentimes the motivation behind seeking money, fame, and power is the misguided notion that these things will ensure we no longer experience suffering. It's not just about physical things though, we also tend to want to change other people and change our circumstances. We mistakenly think that once we can change others, then we'll find lasting happiness. This also includes our desire to want to be liked. Wanting to change others is wanting for life to be other than it is, which is the very definition of suffering.

Aversion is everything that we avoid and don't want in life. Aversion is the opposite approach of desire. It is our habit of thinking that if we can just avoid certain things in life, we will avoid suffering: if we can somehow avoid experiencing the loss of a job, the humiliation of losing at something, the embarrassment of being wrong, etc. We especially want to avoid looking bad. We all have the habit of aversion towards things that we think are going to take away our happiness.

The problem with these three poisons is that they all drive us to look outside of ourselves to try to achieve happiness or avoid suffering. The irony with these things is that the harder we try to avoid self-inflicted suffering (through desire or aversion), the more likely we are to encounter it. Added to that is the fact that all conditions and circumstances are bound to change. This is why we don't find lasting happiness in acquiring the things or achieving the goals we think will bring happiness. The moment we obtain those things, we start to seek something new to make us happy. Happiness is not found outside ourselves, it is only found within. These teachings aren't intended to discourage us from the pursuit of happiness, they're intended to help us understand that happiness is found in the pursuit itself. The 3 poisons represent our habitual reactivity to life's circumstances. There is no freedom in reactivity and since freedom is the only requirement for happiness, we cannot be happy when we are bound by these poisonous perspectives. If we want to be happy, we need to become free from our habitual reactivity and stop trying to change reality into anything other than what it is.

The Third Noble Truth: The Cessation of Suffering

The cause of self-inflicted suffering can be ended. "Cause" is the key word here. It is not suffering that ceases, it's craving. You don't end suffering; suffering is universal. Instead, you end the fixation on what brings us suffering (craving or clinging). The limiting ideas we hold about ourselves, others, and every other experience can be unlearned. We can shine the light of awareness on the distorted understanding we have of reality vs reality as we think it is. In this sense, our spiritual path isn't about acquiring any new knowledge or insight, it's about unlearning the conceptual truths that are keeping us bound and causing us suffering.

The third noble truth teaches us that we don't need to remain in this unsatisfactory state. We can let go of the clinging and attachment that causes us so much suffering. However, this is a tricky concept to grasp because we can't simply do away with clinging by simple force of will. In fact, the moment we desire to no longer cling, we cling to the idea of not clinging. We can't just say, "OK, from now on, I won't cling to anything." Because the causes and conditions that give rise to clinging will still be present. So how do we give up clinging and attachment?

Part of the problem with the idea of "letting go" of this attachment and craving is our idea of what it means to "let go". We tend to think of letting go as a form of renunciation or rejecting something or even casting away. In the Buddhist context, "letting go" means something else. Letting go happens naturally because of insight. This is why meditation, contemplation and investigation are all so important in Buddhism.

We cling to things because we think they will make us happy or keep us safe, but the clinging itself is what causes us to suffer. When we start to see this for ourselves, we can begin to let go. Letting go is an act of liberation rather than a sacrifice.

The Fourth Noble Truth: The Path to End Suffering

The first three truths are the "what". They tell us about the nature of suffering, the source of suffering is craving, and this attachment is the result of a delusional, self-centered perspective. By gaining insight into the nature of reality, and realizing how our own mental habits are causing the problems, the craving naturally falls away (letting go). The fourth noble truth is the "how" and it will address how this process is accomplished.

Instead of fighting to avoid suffering, we can embrace and explore it as part of our experience of existence.

There is a way, or "path," to end the cause of suffering (craving/clinging/attachment). *The path is to let go of our expectations about the way we think things should be, and instead begin to develop an awareness about the way things are.*

We believe that the way we see things is the way they truly are. But as we've seen, our conceptual truths and our desire for the world to be a certain way cloud our vision, so what we think is reality is actually our skewed perspective. That's why it's so important to take time to really look at the way we see things, and to be willing to let go of certain perceptions that seem true but may not be. The way to do this is laid out by the Buddhist teaching, called the Eightfold Path.

Chapter 8: The Eightfold Path

Buddhism teaches that there are eight specific areas of life where we can focus on seeing reality as it is: understanding, intention, speech, action, livelihood, effort, mindfulness and concentration. These eight areas make up what is commonly referred to as the eightfold path. (This is why the common symbol of Buddhism is a wheel with 8 spokes).

The Eightfold Path is not a moral code to be followed. Instead, it's meant to be a guide for specific areas of life where we can experience and discover the nature of reality. In his book *Old Path, White Clouds,* Thich Nhat Hanh tells a story where the Buddha says "I must state clearly that my teaching is a method to experience reality and not reality itself, just as a finger pointing at the moon is not the moon itself. A thinking person makes use of the finger to see the moon. A person who only looks at the finger and mistakes it for the moon will never see the real moon."

Wise Understanding

Wise understanding starts by simply recognizing that what we are seeing might not actually be what is. Imagine walking into a barn and seeing a coiled hose and mistaking it for a snake. In this case, reality does not affect us. The only thing that affects us is the picture of reality that's in our head. We immediately act as though there is a snake and yet, the reality is that there is no snake. Wisdom is like turning on the light in the barn, which reveals that the snake was actually a hose. We must continually seek after wisdom to help us learn to see the world as it really is. There may be many scenarios on our lives where we experience this. We believe someone is a certain way, or certain circumstances seem to be so negative and later we discover that they were not what we thought they were.

Wise Intent

If we want to reduce suffering, we need to be aware of the intention we have with regards to the things we say and do. When our intentions stem from anger or hatred, they are more likely to cause harm than if they stem from happiness or gratitude. When we are reactive, it is very difficult to be mindful of the intent behind our words and actions. It takes practice to become aware of our intentions. You can practice by asking yourself "why?" as you react to things in life. When I'm feeling anger for example, I like to ask myself: "why am I experiencing this emotion?" If I'm being kind to someone, I ask "why?" Is it because I genuinely care about this person or am I trying to gain something out of this interaction? When you become aware of your intentions, you can decide if you need to create new intentions and perhaps let go of the old ones.

Wise Speech

The way we communicate with ourselves and others is an essential part of creating a peaceful and harmonious life. We are social creatures, and communication is the most important part of human relations. Wise speech means communicating with others in a way that doesn't cause harm. This covers not only actual speech, but all forms of communication—writing, texting, emailing, even audio and video. Lying, gossiping, and insulting others is not wise speech, but neither are compliments you don't mean, promises you don't intend to keep, or sucking up to someone you want to impress. Wise speech considers why you say something as much as what you say.

Wise speech does not always have to be pleasant, nor does it need to withhold ideas or opinions out of fear that someone might disagree, but it should be sincere and genuine. Consider the difference between constructive criticism and destructive criticism. The former may be hard to hear, but its goal is to help you become better at what you're doing. The latter only means to cause pain.

Wise Action

Wise action or conduct means doing what is proper and necessary for your situation. While this sometimes includes (and certainly doesn't discourage) a sense of "doing the right thing" in a moral sense, it more closely resembles a guideline for behaving appropriately in any situation. The problem with a set moral code is that morals change and evolve over time. Adhering to the moral code of another place and time, may not be the wisest form of action for our specific time and place. H.L. Mencken says "morality is doing what's right regardless of what you're told. Obedience id doing what you're told regardless of what is right." Ideally, wise understanding, wise thinking, and wise speech give rise to wise action, where your wisdom leads you to behave fittingly in any scenario you enter.

Wise action is not, in other words, a set of rules to be followed to the letter in every situation. Right and wrong are often subjective, especially in different societies and time periods, and what is acceptable in one society or time is often unacceptable in others. Life is continually changing and evolving, therefore wise action is not an absolute thing or a set moral code.

Wise Livelihood

Livelihood has to do with how we make a living, and how we interact with others while on the job. We need to determine for ourselves if what we do for a living is causing more harm or good for ourselves and others. This goes beyond just the type of job or career we have (drug dealer vs doctor), it includes how we interact with our co-workers or customers. Embezzling funds from your employer is an example of unwise livelihood. A doctor may be causing harm by taking bribes from a pharmaceutical company to prescribe a certain medicine over another. Ultimately, it's up to us to make the judgement call regarding the way we make a living. It's a good idea to incorporate wise intent in this process. Perhaps you can ask yourself: "Why am I doing what I'm doing?" Remember, it's not about picking a career or job with the red cross or something like that, it's about doing what you do with the best intent to not cause harm to others regardless of what your job is.

I used to work for a company that sold health supplements. After working there for a while, I became really uncomfortable with one of the sales methods we used on our customers. We would entice them to try the supplement by signing up for a free trial and then they would be enrolled in a monthly subscription for the supplement that they were often unaware of. While I believed in the product itself, I was very uncomfortable with the harm and frustration we were causing to so many people who were not reading the fine print when signing up for their free trial. For me, this job was not a form of wise livelihood for me. I ended up leaving the job and finding another job where I no longer had conflicting feelings about my livelihood.

Wise Effort

Wise effort is what it takes to put into practice all the other parts of the path. It takes effort on our part if we want to experience any kind of positive change on our lives. In order to learn any new skill, whether it be music, sports, business skills, etc., we must have effort. We can usually look at ourselves and recognize if we are giving the proper amount of effort or not. Without effort, there is usually little to no progress. Our effort affects everything we do in the world.

Have you ever set out to accomplish something only to fail? Could it be that effort played a part in that? I have tried to learn to play guitar for over ten years but I've never actually done a good job with it because I've had a hard time with putting in the effort required to do it. I know that the key to accomplishing this goal is effort and yet it's still very difficult for me. I've put in the time and effort into other things that I've wanted to do or accomplish (like writing this book) but the guitar has been hard for me. How much effort do you put into the things you do in life? Relationships, jobs, hobbies, etc. Wise effort is about prioritizing our effort in all the things we do and dedicating the time and effort required to become more mindful and aware of the nature of reality. Without effort, there can be no awakening or enlightenment.

Wise Mindfulness

Wise mindfulness is about paying attention. Being mindful helps us to stay anchored in the present moment. We typically refer to mindfulness as mindfulness practice because it does indeed require practice and effort to become more mindful.

Have you ever been driving somewhere only to realize that you were not really paying attention and you've missed your turn? Maybe you were zoned out? We do this in a lot of areas in life, not just while driving. When we're not mindful, we're not aware, and we miss things that might be right in front of our eyes. This becomes really helpful when it comes to time. When we're stuck with constant thoughts of the past or future it's hard to be mindful of what's happening in the present. Have you ever tried to communicate with someone who was distracted on their smartphone? It can be frustrating to interact with someone who is not present and aware. There is a time and a place for distraction but wise mindfulness is about knowing when and where we should be paying attention.

Wise Concentration

Concentration is the practice of focusing the mind solely on one thing: whatever it is we are doing at that moment. Meditation is a great tool to practice concentration. When we think of meditation we typically think of someone sitting cross-legged on the floor with their eyes closed. Meditation can be much more than just sitting. We can practice meditation while washing the dishes, walking, and doing virtually any activity. Alan Watts says "you can make any human activity into meditation simply by being completely with it and doing it just to do it."

The opposite of wise concentration is distraction. Most of us live in a society where we are constantly bombarded with opportunities for distraction. Whether it's the chime on our smartphones indicating a new email, text, or Facebook update has arrived, or one of thousands of advertisements that compete for our attention virtually everywhere we look, distraction is everywhere. Distraction prevents us from seeing life as it really is. Distraction prevents us from seeing the truth about ourselves and others. In my daily commute to work, I pass by several fields and farms. One day, I decided to ride my bike instead of driving. While rounding the bend in the road, I noticed a red barn behind a cluster of trees out in the field. I had driven past this exact spot for years and I have never noticed that red barn out in the field. Maybe it's because I tend to be distracted while I drive, listening to my music or audiobooks, thinking about work, etc. But this day, I was going slowly and paying attention and I discovered something new that was there all along. What things are waiting to be discovered or seen by simply paying attention?

    The Eightfold Path is not a path we walk only once, or in a particular order. You'll notice how various segments of the path overlap and rely on each other, and how some of them flow into or relate back to each other as well. "Walking the path" is an ongoing practice that can bring about a new sense of awareness and perspective in our lives. Buddhism is often referred to as a practice because you're always practicing to be a better whatever you already are. The Eightfold Path can serve as a guideline for the specific areas of our lives where we can focus on becoming better versions of ourselves.

Chapter 9: Seeing With I's of Wisdom

"The fool who knows he is a fool is that much wiser" - Unknown

When I was 20 years old, I was with a friend and I tried on his glasses, I was quite shocked to discover that I could actually see better. Up until that moment, I didn't know that I needed glasses. It was weird to be able to look at the surrounding mountains and suddenly be able to see details that I didn't know where there. Nothing changed but for me, everything changed because suddenly I was seeing differently, I was seeing clearly. I wore glasses for about 10 years after that and then I eventually got Lasik surgery and I experienced this all over again. I woke up the morning after the surgery and suddenly experienced life in high definition. It was even more crisp and clear than it was with glasses. Sometimes, by changing how we see things, everything changes and suddenly or gradually we can see with much more clarity than before.

Buddhism teaches us that in terms of space, all things are interdependent and in terms of time, all things are impermanent. These two ways of seeing the world are at the heart of the Buddhist worldview. These are the I's (eyes) of wisdom. When we understand that all things are impermanent and all things are interdependent, the way we see things will begin to change.

Interdependence

We tend to see things, including ourselves, as separate and independent entities in relation to everything else. There's me and there's you, but I'm completely independent of you and everything else in the world, and vice versa, right? Well, not exactly. The irony is that we each only exist because of the actions of other people, namely our parents. Were it not for them, we would not be here. Without any effort on our part, causes and conditions were met that resulted in the existence of you, and of me, here and now. This means we are actually *inter*dependent with everything that allows us to exist here and now. This is true of all things. Everything has causes and conditions.

When you look at a car, you might just see a car, an independent object that's separate from everything around it. The reality of the car is that it's dependent on all the parts and processes that allow it to exist. If you were to take a car and disassemble it into all its parts and spread them out in the parking lot, you wouldn't be able to point to which of those parts is the car. Not one single part of the car is the car. A car is the sum of all its parts. You can take anything and break it down to its parts. (Kind of like how all six parts of the elephant weren't actually the elephant.) When we understand this, we start to see things as interdependent rather than independent. We start to see ourselves as interdependent with everything that makes us who we are. We will experience a major shift in how we see the world when we start to understand the nature of interdependence. We are the sum total of all of our parts.

I once heard a Zen story about a child who came home from school upset about being called names on the playground. His father listened carefully to the story and could feel his son's pain and frustration. When his son was done telling him the story, the father picked up a small stick and whacked his son on the hand. The son yelled out, "hey, why did you do that?" The father whacked him again on the hand. The son said, "Why are you doing that? Why did you whack me?" The father then asked him, "are you mad at the stick for whacking you?" "No! I'm mad at you for hitting me with the stick," replied the son. The dad said, "are you mad at my hand for whacking you with the stick? My arm for controlling my hand? My brain for controlling my arm? What are you mad at?" The son realized that what his dad was trying to teach him was that being mad at someone who treated you poorly is like being mad at the stick or the hand, there is always something else behind it. All things have causes and conditions, and those causes and conditions in turn, have their own causes and conditions. How far back do we go in the causes and conditions to find the source of what we're really mad at? And once we do, how important is it to remain angry? This is the lesson of interdependence.

Impermanence

We tend to see things as fixed and permanent. This includes how we see ourselves. This idea of permanence causes a lot of suffering for ourselves and for others.

There is a fable of a powerful king who assembles his sages and asks them to create a ring with a message that will always ring true and will make him happy when he is sad. After careful deliberation, the sages hand him a simple ring with the words "This too shall pass" etched on it. The message had the desired effect to make him happy when he was sad. However, it also had the curse of making him sad whenever he was happy!

The Greek philosopher Heraclitus said, "There is nothing permanent except change." The nature of reality is that all things are constantly changing therefore all things are impermanent. Everything is impermanent. Jobs, relationships, the good times, the bad times, loved ones, our own lives, the lives of everyone we know, literally everything. The problem is that we know this and yet we continue to cling to things as if they were permanent because we want things to last. When we start to understand the nature of impermanence, our tendency to cling to outcomes and expectations will begin to diminish. That doesn't mean its suddenly easy when we lose a job, or a loved one, it just means that the recovery from suffering will go more smoothly when we learn to see things as they really are, impermanent.

    Buddhism teaches the concept of impermanence from two overall perspectives: gross impermanence and subtle impermanence. Gross impermanence is our understanding that things die, people die, empires rise and fall, societal norms change and evolve, the kind of impermanence we see all around us. Like clouds, issues and problems arise, they endure for a while and then they pass away. This gross impermanence is held up by what can be called subtle impermanence. Subtle impermanence is the recognition that all things are changing constantly. At this very moment you are physically undergoing change, cells in your body are dying and regenerating. We should start to think of ourselves and everything around us as sequences of momentary events rather than as single solid things. "This too shall pass" can be applied to all things because all things are impermanent.

    The water in a river is continually flowing and changing, so it's always a new river. The fire from a candle is continually flickering and burning more fuel, so therefore it's constantly a new fire. Life is constantly changing from moment to moment, so therefore it's always a new life, a new experience from moment to moment. All things are constantly changing and evolving...all things are impermanent. When we understand that all things are impermanent, we begin to find that everything is more meaningful. This is an important aspect of the spiritual path, because as you'll remember, finding meaning is one of the two key components of spirituality.

Chapter 10: Awareness and Emptiness

I remember the first time I saw the Grand Canyon, I felt a sense of awe and wonder. I've felt this same thing on occasion simply by looking up at the stars on a clear night. Just thinking of the vastness of the cosmos can evoke this feeling of awe for me. I've certainly felt this sense of awe every time I've experienced holding one of my new born children and looking into their eyes for the first time. Another occasion is when I'm out in nature and just taking it all in.

When we're in nature, we see everything as it is, trees are just trees, flowers are just flowers, rivers are just rivers, there is no pretending, there are no hidden meanings or false pretenses. There are no stories, only reality as it is. In these moments, we feel completely free to be what we are, nature doesn't demand anything of us, we don't get judged for the color of the backpack we're wearing, there are no hidden agendas, we can simply exist in a completely authentic and genuine state. I think that's why we feel so refreshed when we experience nature. Then we go back to social interactions and we lose all that again, we go back into the story of reality and it's no longer the same as reality itself. I think these moments of awe are glimpses of seeing life as it really is, without the stories. *The magic of reality is being able to see life as it is.* And the best part is that we can learn to see and experience this sense of awe and wonder in the most ordinary things. From the Buddhist view, the most simple and ordinary things become extraordinary through awareness.

Awareness

Early on in my Buddhist studies, I came across a Zen story about a strawberry. The story goes like this: There was once a man who was being chased by a ferocious tiger across a field. At the edge of the field there was a cliff. In order to escape the jaws of the tiger, the man caught hold of a vine and swung himself over the edge of the cliff. Dangling down, he saw, to his dismay, there were more tigers on the ground below him! When things seemed like they couldn't get worse, two little mice showed up and started gnawing on the vine to which he clung. He knew that at any moment he would fall to certain death. Just then, he noticed a wild strawberry growing on the cliff wall. Clutching the vine with one hand, he plucked the strawberry with the other and put it in his mouth. He never before realized how sweet a strawberry could taste.

When I first heard this story, I thought "Well, then what?? What happened to him?" And of course, the story never told me. Over time, I've come to understand that it was never about what happens to the man. It's a story about the fact that even in those dire circumstances, this man was capable of maintaining awareness. Awareness of the fact that there was a strawberry next to him, and awareness of just how sweet the strawberry tasted. In our day to day lives, we are somewhat like this man, generally stuck between a rock and a hard place. Struggling to figure out what to do next, in that process of constant reactivity, we have a hard time being aware of the things around us.

On a recent business trip, I was feeling stressed and anxious about a meeting I was going to have with some business partners. There was a lot riding on whether or not this deal I was trying to negotiate would be successful or not. On the day of the meetings, I noticed how tense I was and I thought back to this Zen story of the strawberry. I paused and I asked myself, what am I not aware of? What's going on around me right now that I am not noticing? I stopped walking and I started looking around me in all directions, I took out my camera and I noticed a large flock of birds flying from one tree to another neighboring tree. I captured the video footage of it on my iPhone camera in slow motion. The footage was incredible, because it was so many birds flying in slow motion. To this day, it's one of my favorite videos to watch on my phone. For the next 15-20 minutes, I was enthralled with watching these birds and observing their patterns of behavior and experiencing the beauty of flight and nature.

It was in that moment that I realized what was really being taught in the story of the strawberry. It was not about the outcome or what happens next. It's about being aware of what we are experiencing right here and right now. In this case, I was already prepared for my meeting and the pitch I was going to give and there was nothing more I could do about that but just wait for the meeting and be aware of what was going on around me. When you find yourself stuck between the proverbial rock and hard place, hanging on the side of the cliff, waiting to see what happens next, try to look around and see if there is anything going on that you're not noticing. Remember, even noticing that you're not noticing anything is already a form of awareness. Then, when you drop into that awareness, you may find the strawberry that's right in front of you.

Emptiness

Another important Buddhist concept around the nature of reality is the concept of emptiness. Emptiness can be a difficult concept to understand from a Western mindset. In our culture, we tend to want to have a reason or a meaning for everything. If I'm going to do something, I expect to get something out of it. We go to school to earn a degree so we can use the degree to get a job so that the job will earn us money so we can use the money to buy the things that we think will make us happy. If we go to the gym, it's because we want to be fit or lose weight. There are very few things that we do for the simple sake of just doing them. The understanding of emptiness is that *all things are empty of meaning until we assign meaning to those things*. It's like a blank canvas for a painter. The canvas is always empty and blank, but the painter can come along and create something on that emptiness with paint. Words are a good example of emptiness. Every word you know, a combination of sounds, was completely empty of meaning until someone at some point in history decided that its particular sound should have its particular meaning. If we didn't assign meaning to the sounds we make, they would just be sounds.

From the Buddhist perspective, all things are like this, all things are empty of inherent meaning. This doesn't mean things are meaning*less*, it just means that the meaning things have come from us (the givers of meaning) and not from the things themselves. Things don't come with a meaning, things just are and we are the ones who assign meaning to things.

Remember, there's what is, and then there's the story we create about what is. Reality is simply what is. Life is reality, life is simply what is. We can create stories and make meaning about life just like we tend to do with everything else, but why would we? We don't need to be like the man in the parable of the arrow who was more concerned with the unknowable and unnecessary details of the arrow instead of just facing the situation at hand. The situation at hand is that due to circumstances, there is life. And we get to be a part of it! See, this is where it gets really exciting. Once we learn to see the reality of life, we realize that we are the result of all that is. One of the stories we make about the meaning of life is that we are at the center of it all. All this exists for us. But the truth is that it's the other way around. We only exist because of all that is. We, like all other forms of life, are the result of billions of years of causes and conditions.

This is emptiness. It's the understanding that as life unfolds, it doesn't mean anything...and that's not a positive or a negative thing (who knows what is good and what is bad). All things simply are as they are.

Chapter 11: The Karma of You

"It's not happiness that makes us grateful; it's gratefulness that makes is happy." - Brother David Steindl-rast

Karma

Karma one of the best-known words from the Buddhist vocabulary. It's also very misunderstood. Generally, when you hear the word karma, what comes to mind? Most likely it's something along the lines of "what goes around, comes around," right? It's common to think of karma as a cosmic form of justice, but that's not actually the Buddhist understanding of Karma. I'm sure you've noticed that good things happen to bad people, and bad things happen to good people, so where is the justice? Simply stated, karma is the law of cause and effect within a system of interdependence. EVERYTHING depends on other things (car depends on engine, wheels, steering wheel, etc...). So instead of thinking of it as "if I do something good/bad, I'll get something good/bad," think of it as "if I do something, something will happen." Much like Newton's third law (for every action there is a reaction), karma is simply the law of cause and effect. Rather than thinking of it as "good" or "bad" karma, think of it as just karma.

If you mix the right ingredients in the right order and bake them at the right temperature, you get a cake. If you mix the wrong ingredients, mix up the order, bake at the wrong temperature, you end up with something else. Both things are the result of karma. If you get angry and punch a wall, you may break your hand, and that's karma, too. It is the effect (broken hand) of a cause (you punching the wall).

That being said, once you understand that karma is the law of cause and effect, you can learn to pursue causes that produce positive effects. Being kind to someone else is the classic example, where if you're kind to them, they're either kind back to you or they pay the kindness forward. This is a form of karma. (I'd suggest looking for the effect closer to home, though: kindness also makes the other person happy, makes you feel good, and helps you be a kind person.)

      We exist because of the actions of others. You are the result of karma. Let's talk about the karma of you. The Buddhist teacher Gyomay Kubose sums up this concept up pretty nicely with the expression that "all that I am is the sum total of others." What does that mean? Let's consider for a minute some of the causes and conditions that were required for you to exist. We can start at the very beginning. As far as we know...nearly 14 billion years ago, the universe sprang forth in what scientists call the big bang. Over the course of the next several billion years, as the universe continued to expand, galaxies, stars, and planets began to take shape. Planet earth is estimated to be about 4.5 billion years old and around 3.8 billion years ago, the required circumstances emerged for life to exist. This chain reaction of events is the direct cause of each and every one of us existing today. We exist because of everything. In a very literal way, we are the sum total of everything that exists. This understanding of interdependence can radically deepen our sense of connection to all things. In this incredible vastness of space and time, at some point, you and I came into existence. Through absolutely no effort on our part, we each suddenly became alive and conscious. All because of the actions of others and because of the culmination of all that is and we are each completely unique. In the combination of space and time, there has never been and there will never be another you existing the way you do right here and now. You are a miracle because you are absolutely unique!

Chapter 12: Life Before Death

"We are going to die, and that makes us the lucky ones. Most people are never going to die because they are never going to be born. The potential people who could have been here in my place but who will in fact never see the light of day outnumber the sand grains of Arabia. Certainly those unborn ghosts include greater poets than Keats, scientists greater than Newton. We know this because the set of possible people allowed by our DNA so massively exceeds the set of actual people. In the teeth of these stupefying odds it is you and I, in our ordinariness, that are here. We privileged few, who won the lottery of birth against all odds, how dare we whine at our inevitable return to that prior state from which the vast majority have never stirred?" - Richard Dawkins

Most Western religions have some focus on or aspect of life after death. But from the Buddhist perspective, birth and death are not the beginning and end of life. Death is simply the culmination of the phase that started with birth but the overall process of life started long before and will continue long after our individual birth and death. It's like recognizing that there is music (life) and then there are songs (individuals). While we are songs, with a starting note (birth) and a final note (death), we were never just a song, we are music, and the music goes on. Your life is like the ongoing stream of notes in a song. Every single note, whether you like it or not, is a part of the song. The song is the sum total of all of its notes. The beauty of the song is found in the continual changing of the notes including the eventual final note that marks the end of the song.

For many people, death is a scary thing. Death represents the end of all that is familiar, and we are not comfortable with the unfamiliar music that's beyond the final note in the song we're so used to hearing. But in reality, there is no need to fear death because while death may be the end of the song, it is not the end of the music. So rather than focusing on life after death, we can instead choose to focus on life before death—the life we're living now. Rather than speculating about what happens when we die, what if we could anchor ourselves in the present moment.

What would your world look like if you chose to believe in life before death? Instead of seeing yourself as a limited entity that must experience death, or even a permanent entity that transcends death, you could see yourself as a continually changing entity that's interdependent with everything else (including death). An understanding of impermanence and interdependence can ease the fear of death by reminding us that birth wasn't the start and death isn't the end. There is no beginning and there is no end, there is only change. The death of a caterpillar is the birth of a butterfly. Every beginning has an end and every end gives birth to a new beginning.

We feel such a strong sense of self and identity. The reality is that we are made up of a lot of impermanent things that just feel permanent: our name, memories, relationships, jobs, possessions, beliefs, etc. What is there about us that is permanent? There is nothing.

When the building blocks of our identity are removed, what do we have left? We have an empty person that we do not know. We've been living with ourselves, like a stranger for a roommate that we've never actually met.

When we fear death, we seek comfort by distracting ourselves from the certainty of death. We accumulate things, and we spend a mind-numbing amount of time watching TV and staring at our phones and doing anything we can to distract ourselves from the reality of life and from suffering or discomfort. Then when death comes, as it eventually does to ourselves or to someone we love, oh the misery and despair. We say "how could this happen?" But really, how could it *not* happen? It's the one certain thing we can all plan on!

A few years ago, my good friend and business partner taught me a wonder lesson about life. He was diagnosed with stage 4 melanoma and was told he only had a few months to live. As his condition deteriorated, I asked him "what does it feel like to know you're dying?" He just looked at me, grinned, and said "I don't know, you tell me! You're dying too." His reply reminded me that I could be in an accident on my drive home, or have an aneurysm, or have some unexpected thing happen to me when I least expect it. He was right; we were both dying; We all are.

Buddhism teaches that thinking about death is a wise way to live. We can actually use our lives to prepare for death. We don't need to spend our lives meditating in a cave to do this. And we don't have to wait for the painful experience of losing someone we love, or even getting a terminal diagnosis ourselves, to shock us into living. We can begin here and now to make life meaningful by understanding that meaning isn't out there waiting to be found, it's in you, waiting to be created. Bronnie Ware was a palliative nurse who spent years working with patients who were dying. She recorded their most common regrets and published her findings in a book called "The Top Five Regrets of the Dying". The top five regrets she encountered were: "I wish I'd had the courage to live a life true to myself, not the life others expected of me." "I wish I hadn't worked so hard." "I wish I'd had the courage to express my feelings." I wish I had stayed in touch with friends and family." And "I wish I had let myself be happier." I think it's fascinating that many people did not realize until the end that happiness is a choice.

Buddhism teaches us that there is no need for regret. The present moment is the result of the past and it can't be changed. We only experience regret when we compare the present moment as it is to how we think the present moment should be.

Every moment is an experience we've never had before and will never have again. The uniqueness of each moment is what makes it beautiful. We tend to think that the beauty of a moment is found in whether or not it is a happy or enjoyable moment, but with our new understanding of impermanence, we can now see that every moment is unique, and thus every moment is beautiful. Whether it's happy or sad or downright miserable, it is still beautiful.

My wife and I recently had our third child, a baby girl. I remember the moment she was born, I was instantly flooded with emotions and suddenly I was thinking about all my hopes and dreams for her. I was looking into her eyes imagining what she'll be like and what her sense of humor would be like and what will she be when she grows up, etc. Then in that same moment, I had a terrible thought. What if she gets sick? (She was born during flu season.) I started to picture her with tubes in her nose and needles in her arms. Then the most amazing thing happened. I paused my reactive thinking and was able to just be present with her. I stared into her little eyes and I just enjoyed the moment. I knew there was no certainty about what tomorrow or even later that day would bring, but I was certain that in that moment, I was experiencing a miracle. I was experiencing the present, a moment that has never been and will never be again and it felt like pure magic!

We live life moment by moment, with the certainty of uncertainty because the present moment is all we'll ever have. This includes the moments that are happy and the moments that are sad and moments where we feel anger or compassion, they are all just moments, completely unique and precious because each moment is a moment that we've never had.

Consider a rose, it grows in the field when

the conditions are right and it simply exists, in all its beauty and splendor. It doesn't wait around for someone to come pluck it and tell it that it's beautiful. It's beautiful because it is just doing what a rose does, it's being a rose, without any story or meaning. That's what makes it beautiful. And so it is with life, it springs up when the conditions are right and without any effort on our part, we suddenly exist. 14 billion years of non-existence and then boom, here we are! And yet it's only for a fraction of a sliver of time and then just as the rose, the petals fall and, we're gone. And somehow in that blink of an eye, if we're lucky, we get to experience what it feels like to love, to laugh, to cry, to hurt, to feel. What a miracle! How could we not feel anything but gratitude for the experience of being alive?

As we reach this understanding of our own karma, the impermanence of our lives, and the miracle of the present moment, we will learn to live without regrets. We will start to live our lives in a way that will bring us joy because of our sense of gratitude. We will be more present for ourselves and for the people we care about and this will bring them more happiness and joy.

Chapter 13: Becoming Who You Are

"My mother said to me, 'If you are a soldier, you will become a general. If you are a monk, you will become the Pope.' Instead, I was a painter, and became Picasso." – Pablo Picasso

Discovering Yourself

"The privilege of a lifetime is being who you are." – Joseph Campbell

Of all the things that Picasso could have become, he became himself. This teaching is as the heart of what Buddhism teaches about the self. Of all the goals we can aspire to be, we serve ourselves and the world best when we aspire to discover and become exactly who we are. The problem is, when we get caught up in the image in our minds of how life is supposed to be rather than just letting it be what it is, we also do this with our sense of self. We get caught up in the mental image of how we think we're supposed to be and this limits us from being free to just be who we are.

Buddhism is a path of liberation. A path that allows us to be free from the stories that prevent us from seeing reality as it is. Remember, in order to be open to seeing reality, we must first doubt the assumptions we've made about reality. Remember my story at the beginning of the book about not being able to see Chris? I had an image in my mind of what Chris was supposed to be (a man) and that literally prevented me from seeing what Chris really was (a woman). When we doubt our assumptions, only then are we open to whatever might be. The nature of faith is to have an attitude of being open to whatever might be and the nature of doubt is to be cautious about the assumptions we make that might be blinding us from seeing reality as it is.

We are Not Our Labels

As we learn to see reality as it really is, the most difficult thing to see will be ourselves. We're perpetually caught up in the lie of "I". The lie of independence. The idea that we exist as independent beings, separate from others, is a great source of suffering. One of the most difficult and dangerous ways that suffering shows up is in the labels and titles we add to ourselves. These labels alter the way we see ourselves, so we can no longer see ourselves as we really are. Instead of simply seeing ourselves as "myself," we take on all kinds of labels and start seeing them as our identities.

The thing is, labels never define the reality of myself, because they represent who I think I am, not who I actually am. More than that, labels are as impermanent as anything else. Even the most harmful ones, we outgrow and move away from with time and mindfulness and presence. Labels are temporary indications of HOW we are, but never permanent indications of WHO we are. I like to remind myself of this impermanence by imagining my labels as articles of clothing. When I wear a blue shirt, the shirt is an indicator of how I am at the moment, "the guy in the blue shirt," but it's never who I am. The labels we carry throughout life are temporary and impermanent. My label of "college student" only lasted about 4 years. I've had many labels: father, son, brother, husband, student, teacher, American, tourist, business owner, pilot, etc., none of which will last longer than my own existence. When I interact with others, it's helpful for me to also see their labels as articles of clothing. I can see someone wearing an orange shirt, and I can understand that they are not their shirt—even while also seeing them, temporarily, as "the person in the orange shirt." What labels do you give yourself? What labels do you use on others? What would they look like without the labels you've given them? What would you look like without the labels you've given yourself?

Letting Go

"A thought is harmless unless we believe it. It's not our thoughts, but our attachment to our thoughts, that causes suffering." - Byron Katie

The famous Zen master Thich Nhat Hanh says: "Letting go gives us freedom and freedom is the only condition for happiness." If we want to experience lasting happiness, we have to be willing to let go. We must have the attitude of faith in being open to whatever might be. So much of our suffering in life comes from the distorted image in our heads of how we think life should be. What would your life look like if you learned to let it go?

There is a famous Buddhist parable in which a man who comes to encounter a large body of water while on his journey. Seeing that there is now way to cross it, be begins the task of building a raft. He dedicates a significant amount of time and energy into building the raft. Once he completes the building of the raft, he continues his journey by floating on the raft to cross the water. His careful efforts pay off as his raft is able to get him safely across the water. Once on the other side, his journey continues on dry land. The Buddha stops the story at this point and he asks the monks, if it would be wise for this man to continue the journey with the raft on should it be left behind? After so much time and energy dedicated to raft, it would be difficult to simply leave it behind, however it would also be unwise to continue the journey with a heavy raft on his back. The consensus among the monks is that it would be wiser to leave the raft behind. The journey will be easier without the raft. I like to imagine this parable has application to the beliefs and the conceptual truths that we so carefully build while on the journey of life. At some point on the journey, the raft will no longer be necessary and at that moment, we need to decide if we should continue to carry it on our back or to have the wisdom to let it go. We each have rafts in the form of thoughts, ideas, relationships, beliefs, and more that may have been useful at some point on our spiritual journey but now they are just useless weight that we continue to carry on our backs. In fact, they may be hindering the progress we can make because they add unnecessary weight to our load. Your journey can change drastically if you can learn to let go!

But letting go is not easy. Sometimes, we think we've let go of the raft, only to find that we are still tethered to it dragging it through the dirt as we struggle to find the reason why our journey is so difficult and hard. There is another famous Zen story of two monks who are on a journey through the forest. On their journey they come across a river that needs to be crossed. Standing at the edge of the river, they see a young woman in her wedding dress trying to figure out how to cross without ruining her dress. Without giving it much through, the senior monk picks up the woman in her arms and carries her across the water, gently putting her down on the other side. She thanks the monk and the continue on their way. The junior monk can't believe what he's seen. He recalls the vows that he took as a young monk to "never touch a woman". As they continue their journey, the thought continues to linger for the junior monk and it starts to drive him mad. Finally, after hours of traveling, the junior monk finally speaks up and says "How could you? How is it that you made a sacred vow to never touch a woman and yet you picked up that young woman at the river and carried her as if it was nothing?" The senior monk calmly replied "I put that woman down on the other side of the river...why do you continue to carry her?" Sometimes we are like the junior monk and we have limiting ideas, concepts, and beliefs that we continue to carry around even though we think we left them behind long ago.

    We can pause and evaluate our own lives right now and we can make the mindful decision to let go of our unnecessary rafts. Regardless of how important these were for us in the past, regardless of how much time and energy we invested in these rafts, we can simply let them go and lighten the load off our shoulders. Then we can make sure that we really did let them go and that we're not still carrying them like the woman across the river. Just let them go and continue the journey.

Conclusion

"My religion is to live, and die, without regret." – Milarepa

Our minds have two basic positions: looking outward and looking inward. Buddhist teachings aim at helping us to learn to look inward, to look into the nature of the mind, and to liberate us from our ideas and concepts, especially our limiting beliefs that are the source of so much of our self-inflicted suffering. Looking in is very difficult. We are so addicted to looking outside ourselves for peace and happiness, that we don't even realize that we've made our lives so hectic and distracted that it's virtually impossible to look in. In our pursuit of happiness, we've overlooked the fact that happiness can be found in the pursuit itself. When we live with continual distraction, peace and contentment will always elude us.

When we learn to look in we awaken to one of the key teachings found in Buddhism: that we are already perfect. We always have been.

Alan Watts used to ask: "Have you ever seen a misshapen cloud?" Of course not, because a cloud is just a cloud and there is no right or wrong way for the cloud to be. A cloud is perfect because it is perfectly a cloud. In this same sense, we are perfect just as we are because we are perfectly what we are. The problem we run into is that we compare who we are vs who we think we should be and then the idea of being perfect becomes impossible to understand. The reason many people struggle with the idea of perfection is because they have already formulated an idea of what perfect is (or isn't). Remember when I was in China looking for Chris? I couldn't see Chris because I had an idea in my mind of who Chris was and that idea prevented me from seeing Chris. When you awaken to this truth, suddenly life looks different. It's not that life changed, it's that the way we see life changed and that changes everything! Our true nature and the nature of all beings is not something extraordinary, it is unexpectedly ordinary and ordinarily perfect!

    I shared a quote by Thich Nhat Hanh at the beginning of the book that I also want to end with: "The secret of Buddhism is to remove all ideas, all concepts, in order for the truth to have a chance to penetrate, to reveal itself." Living a mindful, awakened life is much like playing at the beach with young children who are building a sand castle. Even if they start fighting over who's turn it is to use the shovel, or complaining that their wall or tower was stepped on, or whatever form of drama may arise for them, you don't feel the same level of anxiety or drama over the sand castle because you know that in the end, a wave will come and wash it away. It's impermanent. That's how we start to see life, we start to thoroughly enjoy the experience of living because we start to glimpse just how fragile, short, and perfect life is. We can enjoy every aspect of our impermanent nature, the times we feel good AND the times we feel bad, they are both part of the beautiful experience of being human.

Try removing the ideas and concepts you have about people and situations in your life and see what happens. Perhaps you will suddenly see something that was there all along but you were blind to it all this time. This is what it means to be awake, to be capable of seeing ourselves and others as we see the clouds—perfect shapes that are constantly changing and interdependent with their environment. Many people will spend their whole lives looking for happiness outside of themselves only to discover that it was to be found inside the whole time. We wake up when we discover for ourselves that everything we needed to be happy was right here all along. I hope you can take several of these teachings and concepts into your own life and you can experience this sense of awakening. My wish is for you to be free from self-inflicted suffering and to have joy.

May it be so.

Lightning Source UK Ltd.
Milton Keynes UK
UKHW011831301218
334695UK00012B/292/P